MISSION SURVIVAL:
SAVING EARTH'S ENDANGERED ANIMALS

SAVING THE RHINO

SARAH EASON

CHERITON
CHILDREN'S BOOKS

Published in 2026 by **Cheriton Children's Books**
1 Bank Drive West, Shrewsbury, Shropshire SY3 9DJ, UK

First Edition

Author: Sarah Eason
Designer: Paul Myerscough
Editor: Jane Brooke
Proofreader: Ella Newby
Consultant: David Hawksett, BSc

Picture credits: Cover: Shutterstock/HPH Image Library. Inside: pp4-5: Shutterstock/Papa Bravo, pp6-7: Shutterstock/Andy Dean Photography, p7a: Shutterstock, p7b: Shutterstock/Svietlieisha Olena, p7c: Shutterstock/Usmanify, p7d: Shutterstock/Eric Isselee, p9: Shutterstock/Spiks, pp10-11: Shutterstock/HPH Image Library, pp12-13: Shutterstock/Simon Eeman, p13b: Shutterstock/AndreSwanepoel, p13c: Shutterstock/3owaldi, p15: Shutterstock/Marcel Brekelmans, pp16-17: Shutterstock/Euroscript AB, p17b: Shutterstock/Cast Of Thousands, p17c: Shutterstock/Cast Of Thousands, pp18-19: Shutterstock/Muratart, p20: Shutterstock/Henk Bogaard, p21b: Shutterstock/Nisansala99, p21c: Shutterstock/Alexwilko, p21t: Shutterstock/AfricanSunProductions, pp22-23: Shutterstock/Elizabeth Grieb, p23c: Shutterstock/VH-studio, p23t: Shutterstock/VH-studio, pp24-25: Shutterstock/Snap2Art, p26: Shutterstock/Four Oaks, p27b: Shutterstock/Volodymyr Burdiak, p27c: Shutterstock/Four Oaks, p27t: Shutterstock/Rudi Hulshof, pp28-29: Shutterstock/Marcel Blanc, p28b: Shutterstock/TR STOK, p29c: Shutterstock/Lopolo, p29t: Shutterstock/Lopolo, pp30-31: Shutterstock/Diganta Talukdar, pp30-31t: Shutterstock/Naeblys, pp32-33: Shutterstock/Peter van Dam, p32b: Shutterstock/Lozicshrestha Photography, p33c: Shutterstock/Oksana Sahinoglu, p33t: Shutterstock/Johannes Kraak, pp34-35: Shutterstock/Poket Idol, p35b: Shutterstock/Tom Wang, p35c: Shutterstock/Tom Wang, p35t: Shutterstock/JIAHUI LOU, pp36-37: Shutterstock/Vaclav Sebek, p36: Shutterstock/Punghi, p38b: Shutterstock/Danny Ye, p38t: Shutterstock/Nicola K Photos, p39: Shutterstock/Sergei25, pp40-41: Shutterstock/Henrico Muller, p41b: Shutterstock/Xavier Lorenzo, p41c: Shutterstock/Xavier Lorenzo, p42: Shutterstock/Pearl Media, p43b: Shutterstock/Angela Compagnone, p44: Shutterstock/AlvaroGO, p45: Shutterstock/Shyntartanya.

Printed in China

Publisher's Note: The information in the Kids on a Mission features in this book are suggestions for actions that children can take to help protect endangered animals, based on extensive research by the author and consultant. The email addresses and the children featured in the photographs are for illustrative purposes only.

CONTENTS

RHINOS IN DANGER

Rhinos have lived on Earth for millions of years. The first types of rhino appeared on the planet about 50 million years ago. Rhinos once roamed Asia, Africa, Europe, and even North America. However, today rhino numbers have significantly reduced. These animals are now in great danger.

THE BIGGEST THREAT TO RHINOS

There are many threats to rhinos today and most of them are the result of human activity. Rhinos are **poached** for their horns, which are highly valued in some countries. The animals have also lost their natural habitat because of deforestation. That is the cutting down of large areas of forest. They have also lost land to farming and the building of towns. Rhinos are often seen as a threat to farmers too because they can damage crops, which are plants grown for food. That has led to rhinos being hunted and killed. **Climate change** is also a problem for the animals, and is placing them in increasing danger.

The International Union for **Conservation** of Nature (IUCN) keeps a record of the world's **species** and how at risk of **extinction** they are. It is called the **Red List.**

There are more than **46,000** animal species on the List.

Rhinos are among the most at risk, with some species listed as **critically endangered.**

DISAPPEARING FAST

As humans clear rhino **territory**, it breaks it up into small and unconnected areas. That makes it more difficult for rhinos to meet and mate. Rhinos reproduce, or have young, very slowly. A female rhino can be pregnant for about 16 to 18 months. Females give birth to just one calf per pregnancy. That means rhinos cannot quickly recover as their numbers are lost. And because damage to their habitat makes it more difficult for them to meet and mate, the number of rhinos on Earth is getting smaller.

▲ The rhino is an incredible animal. It deserves our respect and our protection.

HELP THE RHINO

Although some rhino species have gone forever and are now extinct, there is still hope for remaining rhinos. It is not too late to save them. People everywhere have learned about rhinos and their need for protection. They are making it their mission to help these amazing animals survive. In this book, we'll learn about the rhino and why it is in danger. We'll discover what people are doing to help rhinos and how they have built a career in conservation. We'll find out how kids on a mission are saving the rhino, and what you can do to help. And we'll learn how you could make a career in conservation your mission. Feeling mission-ready? Then read on!

> "Rhinos ... are symbols of strength, and the beauty of the natural world."
>
> Dereck Joubert, filmmaker and cofounder of the Big Life Foundation

CHAPTER ONE

MEET THE RHINO

With their powerful bodies and magnificent horns, rhinos are immediately recognizable. The animals are well designed for their **environment**. Their bodies are also built for defence. Few hunting animals dare take on an adult rhino.

BIG AND ROUND

The rhino has a huge body with a broad chest. It has very strong bones and large, powerful muscles. Rhinos are some of the largest animals on land. In fact, only the elephant is bigger than the rhino. White rhinos are the biggest of all rhinos. They weigh around 5,000 pounds (2,300 kg) but can weigh up to 7,940 pounds (3,600 kg). Sumatran rhinos are the smallest. They typically weigh up to 1,800 pounds (800 kg).

THAT AMAZING HORN!

As well as being enormous, rhinos are unmistakable because of the huge horn on their head. A rhino's horn is made of a tough material called keratin. Some rhinos have one horn, others have two. The white rhino and the black rhino both have two horns. The front horn is bigger than the back horn. The Sumatran rhino also has two horns, but they are smaller and more rounded. The Indian rhino and Javan rhino both have a single horn.

A VERY TOUGH SKIN

Rhinos have thick, leathery skin that can range in color. Some rhinos are grayish-brown. Others are light gray. Yet others are dark brown. Rhinos that live in Asia tend to have skin with deep folds, especially around the neck and shoulders. African rhinos have smoother skin.

SHORT, STURDY, AND SPEEDY

Short, powerful legs support the rhino's huge body. Each foot has three toes. While rhino legs are short and thick, they do the job of holding up the animal's bulky body. Rhinos typically walk slowly, but can run very quickly in short bursts.

SIGHT, HEARING, AND SMELL

Rhinos have little eyes. The animals do not have good eyesight, but they can smell and hear very well. Their large ears can swivel to catch sounds from different directions. That helps them keep track of predators. Rhinos can pick up scents over large distances too. The part of their brain that processes information about smell is also especially well developed. The animals use this super **sense** of smell to detect threats such as predators. Predators are animals that hunt and eat other animals. The rhino's sense of smell also helps it figure out what other rhinos are nearby.

In a Group

Scientists group animals to help them classify, or order, them. Rhinos belong to a group of animals called *Perissodactyla*, which includes animals with an uneven number of toes on their feet. Within this group are horses, zebras, donkeys, and tapirs.

WHERE RHINOS LIVE

Rhinos live in different parts of Africa and Asia. Some live in open **grassland**. Others are found in **wetlands** and **rain forests**. Rhinos seek out environments that have water for drinking and wallowing in. Wallowing is when an animal rolls in mud and muddy water. Rhinos also look for places that have thick **vegetation**, which can provide calves with protection from predators.

LIVING IN GRASSLANDS

Some species of rhino thrive in grasslands. There they feed on many different grasses. The large, wide-open landscapes provide them with plenty of land in which to roam and search for food. Grasslands also have water for drinking and wallowing. Species such as the white rhino are found in grasslands in Africa. The Indian rhino also lives in grassland, but in Asia.

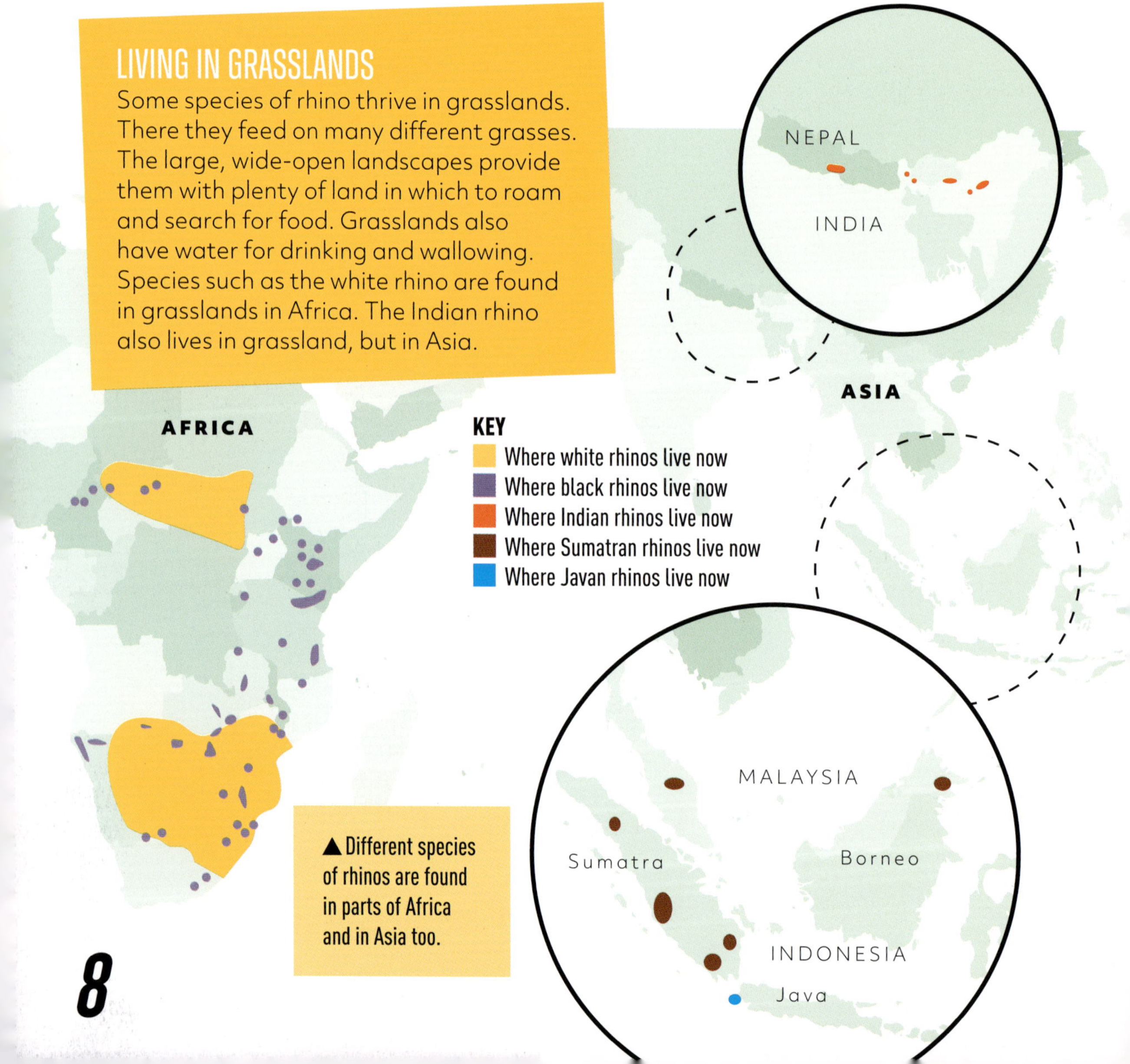

▲ Different species of rhinos are found in parts of Africa and in Asia too.

SCRUBLAND AND WOODLAND

Black rhinos are more often found in **scrubland** and woodland, but can be found in grassland too. These animals like places with thick vegetation. They eat leaves, shrubs, and bushes. Scrubland and woodland provide some protection from predators, too.

▼ Javan rhinos are found in thick, **tropical** rain forests.

WETLAND AND RAIN FOREST RHINOS

Indian rhinos are usually found in wetlands, as well as grasslands. They often live near riverbanks and **swamps**. These animals love wallowing. Doing so helps keep them cool and protects their skin from the sun. Indian rhinos are also found in forests. Sumatran rhinos prefer tropical forests and swamps. They love wallowing in mud, and hide beneath thick vegetation. The Javan rhino mainly lives in thick, hilly rain forests. It likes areas near rivers and swamps, which provide easy hiding places for the animal.

MOVING AROUND

Rhinos live in an area of land that is called their home range. This is a zone that they roam and defend as their territory. Male rhinos tend to have larger home ranges than females. The home ranges of females may overlap a little. Males fiercely defend their home ranges from other males. Rhinos move around their home ranges every day, searching for food and water. They may travel several miles a day. If food is harder to find, during dry seasons for example, they will keep to a smaller home range. During wet seasons, when more food is available over a wider area, the animals travel farther.

WHY SHOULD WE HELP THE RHINO?

Rhinos are often called "ecosystem engineers." That is because they help maintain the health of the ecosystems in which they live. Rhino behavior plays a key part in the environment, and helps many other **organisms** survive there. For that reason, rhinos are called a keystone species.

What Is an Ecosystem?

An ecosystem is a group of natural parts that all work together for a purpose. Ecosystems include nonliving things, such as water, sunshine, and air. These are called abiotic factors. Ecosystems also include living things, such as plants and animals. These are called biotic factors. The living things in an ecosystem depend on the abiotic factors in the ecosystem to survive. Every part of the ecosystem has an important part to play. A healthy ecosystem has many different plants and animals living together. If any part of that ecosystem changes or is damaged, the other parts are affected, too.

Rhinos are incredibly important ▶ to their environments. These super feeders help maintain the health of ecosystems that would otherwise suffer without them.

ENGINEERING BY EATING

Rhinos graze, or feed, on grasses, shrubs, and trees. By doing so, they help keep those plants under control. That allows space for other plants to grow. It results in a more diverse, or varied, range of vegetation. A wide variety of vegetation is important for a healthy ecosystem. The different plants provide food for a lot of different plant-eating animals. Those plant eaters then provide food for a wide variety of meat-eating animals. A diverse ecosystem, with many different types of plants and animals in it, has a greater chance of survival than a narrower ecosystem.

BUILDING HEALTHY HABITATS

Rhino grazing also clears areas of very thick vegetation. That creates more open spaces, such as grasslands. Animals that need those environments then thrive. Rhinos also help create particular types of habitats that some animals need. For example, rhinos build muddy pits. Those muddy areas can then be used by other animals, like birds that need such environments. Rhinos also help plant growth. When they eat plants, the seeds of those plants pass through the animals' digestive system. That is the parts of the body that break down food. The seeds are then dropped onto the ground in dung, or waste. The dung is dropped in different places. The seeds then grow in those different places. That encourages greater plant growth over a wider area.

RHINO MEALTIMES

Rhinos are big eaters! These large animals need to eat a lot every day. Rhinos are plant eaters. Their diet is made up of the type of plants that are available in their habitats.

ON THE MENU

White rhinos mainly eat grasses, which are found in the open grasslands where they live. These animals can eat huge quantities of grass every day—up to 150 pounds (68 kg)! Indian rhinos eat leaves and shoots of shrubs and trees. They also eat grass, herbs, and other plants. Javan and Sumatran rhinos eat mainly leaves and fruit from trees and shrubs. Black rhinos eat more types of plants than any other rhino. They can feed on more than 200 different species of plant.

DESIGNED TO DIGEST

The digestive system of a rhino is designed for breaking down plant matter. It contains microbes, which are tiny organisms. The microbes break down the rough parts of plants as they pass through the digestive system. That helps rhinos extract, or take out, as many nutrients as possible from the food. Nutrients are things in food that are needed for good health, such as vitamins and minerals.

RIPPING AND GRINDING

Rhinos have big mouths that are broad and flat. That helps them work their way quickly through large areas of grass and other vegetation. They pull up lots of plant material in one chomp! Some rhinos also have a **prehensile** upper lip, such as the black rhino. That allows them to grasp onto leaves and branches and pull at them easily. Rhinos also have very strong jaws with powerful muscles. They use them to pull up grasses or chop off chunks of plants. Their teeth are tough and strong, too. They can easily grind up tough plant material. That helps these large animals digest their food.

KNOWING WHERE TO LOOK

Rhinos get to know their home ranges well, and where to find food within them. They often visit places that are rich in the plants they like to eat. They use their good sense of smell to sniff out food too. Some rhinos search for food in small groups, especially mothers with calves. White rhinos more often search for food in groups than other species.

PEOPLE ON A MISSION

Today, more people are aware of the threats rhinos face. That is thanks to conservation organizations that have spread awareness about the dangers to these animals. Many people are so concerned about rhinos that they have made it their mission to help save them.

▼ These rangers are caring for young rhinos that have lost their mothers. The rhinos live in a protected area in Kenya, Africa.

PEOPLE ON THE GROUND

Rangers and anti-poaching units work on the ground to help protect rhinos. They patrol areas in which rhinos live, looking out for poachers. They track rhinos and monitor their health. They may also work in national parks and wildlife reserves, in which rhinos are protected and can live without threat. In some cases, people working to protect rhinos may move them from a location in which they are in danger to a safer place, such as a reserve. It is also the job of **conservationists** on the ground to protect and restore rhino habitat.

PEOPLE IN OFFICES

Protecting rhinos needs the combined efforts of communities, governments, and conservation organizations. Conservation organizations work with the governments of countries in which rhinos live. They put in place stronger laws to protect the animals. **Communications** and public relations experts work to raise awareness about the animals. Rhinos have gathered the help of famous people, who have supported efforts to save the rhino. That has created even more awareness about the dangers the animals face.

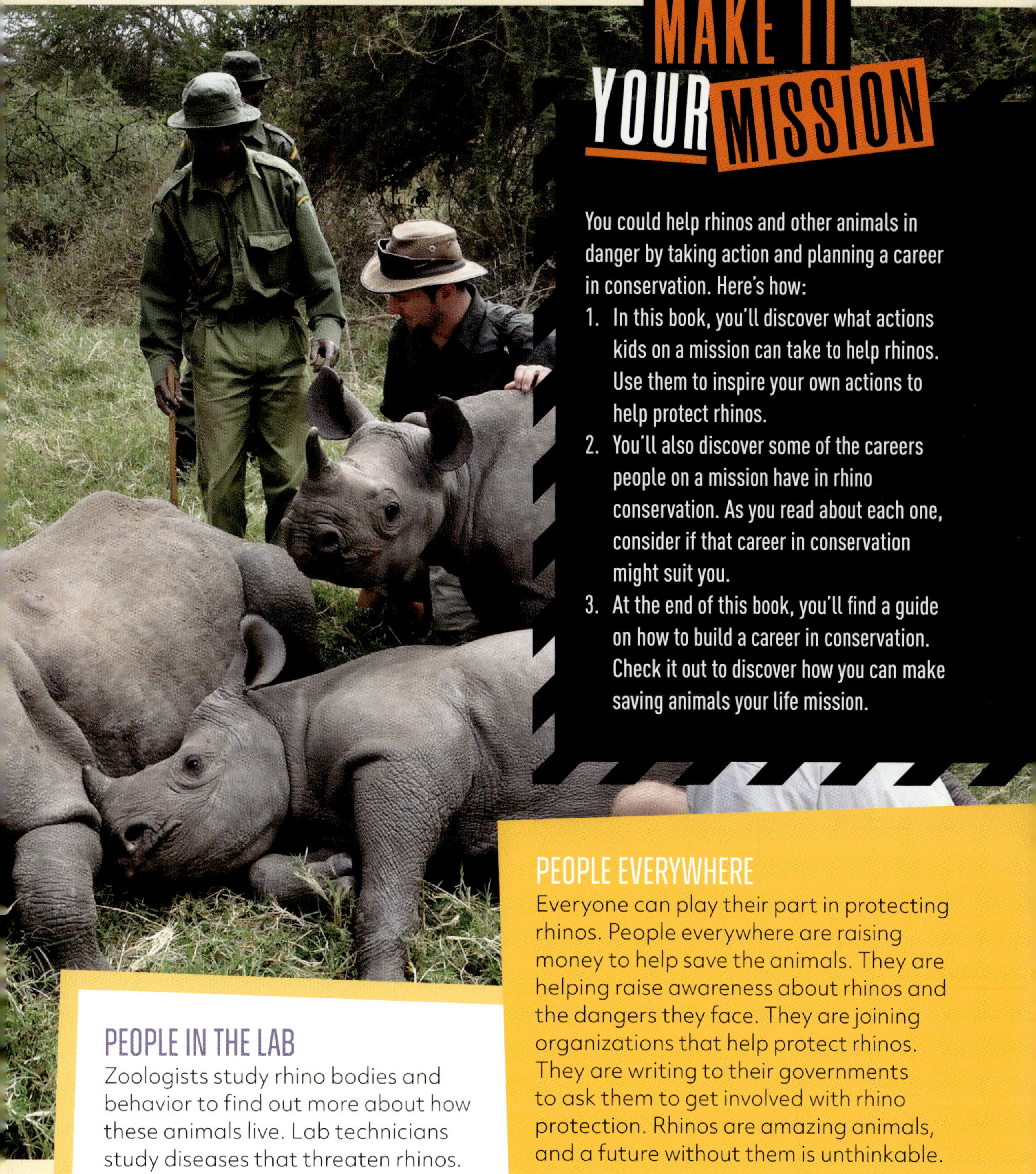

MAKE IT YOUR MISSION

You could help rhinos and other animals in danger by taking action and planning a career in conservation. Here's how:

1. In this book, you'll discover what actions kids on a mission can take to help rhinos. Use them to inspire your own actions to help protect rhinos.
2. You'll also discover some of the careers people on a mission have in rhino conservation. As you read about each one, consider if that career in conservation might suit you.
3. At the end of this book, you'll find a guide on how to build a career in conservation. Check it out to discover how you can make saving animals your life mission.

PEOPLE IN THE LAB

Zoologists study rhino bodies and behavior to find out more about how these animals live. Lab technicians study diseases that threaten rhinos. They also study how rhinos reproduce.

PEOPLE EVERYWHERE

Everyone can play their part in protecting rhinos. People everywhere are raising money to help save the animals. They are helping raise awareness about rhinos and the dangers they face. They are joining organizations that help protect rhinos. They are writing to their governments to ask them to get involved with rhino protection. Rhinos are amazing animals, and a future without them is unthinkable.

CHAPTER TWO

HOMES UNDER THREAT

Rhinos depend on their habitats for food and water. They also need them for safe places in which to reproduce and raise their young. But rhino habitats are under threat mainly due to human activity.

RHINO LAND LOSSES

The number of people on Earth is constantly growing. And as the human **population** gets bigger, people need more land on which to live and grow food. That has resulted in the clearing of land to make room for farmland, villages, towns, and cities. That is often land that rhinos live on. This is a big problem in both Africa and Asia. Not only does the construction of buildings threaten rhino habitats, so too does the building of roads and railroads. Both cut through rhino territory.

▲ These rhinos live in Nairobi National Park in Kenya, Africa. The capital city of Nairobi can be seen in the background.

WORRIES ABOUT WATER

Rhinos need water. They use it for both cooling down in high temperatures and for drinking. However, people are using water sources that rhinos need for their own purposes. They are using it to provide water for their livestock, or farm animals. They are also using it to water crops. When people use too many of these natural water sources, there is not enough left for rhinos. In times when water is hard to find, such as periods of drought, that can lead to rhino deaths.

MOVED TO SAFE PLACES

Threats to rhinos and their habitats are so great that safe places in which the animals can live have been created. These include rhino reserves. The areas are enclosed to stop people getting in. They are patrolled regularly to protect the animals from threats such as poaching. Today, many countries in which rhinos are in danger are setting aside more land for reserves. They are doing so to try and make sure rhinos have enough territory in which to live and reproduce.

@jasmine_helprhinos_109

I want a world full of rhinos, so I'm raising awareness about them. My family supports a rhino protection organization, and every year we donate money to help save rhinos.

"Saving rhinos is... about ***preserving*** *an ecosystem ... for future generations."*

Dr Jane Goodall, conservationist and zoologist

SPOTLIGHT ON FARMING

Increasing amounts of farming in and around rhino territory is affecting their food supply, as well as their supply of water. Farming also brings **pollution** to places populated by rhinos, which is harmful to their health.

▼ Water sources are precious for rhinos and other wildlife, such as zebras. If farmers use too many important resources, these wild animals may die.

TAKING RHINO TERRITORY

When large areas of land are cleared for farming, rhinos are forced into smaller and smaller territories. That means they have fewer resources. That often forces rhinos to roam into farmland in search of food and water. That brings them into contact with farmers. Many farmers see the animals as a threat. That is because they can damage crops as they trample across them in search of food and water. This can often lead to conflict, or violent clashes, between farmers and rhinos. Farmers may harm or kill rhinos to try to drive them off their cropland.

PEOPLE ON A MISSION: WORKING WITH FARMERS

Public education officers and outreach workers play an important role in working with local farming communities. They educate them about rhinos. They talk to farmers about their farming practices. They try to figure out ways that the farmers can protect their crops and farmland while still helping the rhinos. People working in conservation will explain to farmers that rhinos are a keystone species that help maintain healthy habitats. They describe how that benefits the wildlife. Outreach workers also show farmers how they can prevent rhinos getting into fields by using natural barriers. Those might be thorny bushes, for example. By putting those methods in place, conflicts between rhinos and farmers are reduced.

Public education officers will also work with farmers to introduce sustainable farming practices. Those are ways of farming that do not harm the natural environment and wildlife. That might include growing different types of crops and making sure the soil is cared for. It also means using natural methods of controlling pests that eat crops. These sustainable practices help improve the productivity of farms. That means they can produce more crops within a smaller area. As a result, farmers do not need to take as much rhino territory for farmland.

DANGER AND DISEASE

When rhinos meet with livestock, that can endanger them in another way. Livestock may carry diseases that are dangerous to rhinos. For example, cattle can carry bovine tuberculosis, which is a disease that affects an animal's breathing. If rhinos come into contact with livestock such as cattle, they can catch diseases. Those diseases can then spread through entire rhino populations. They can lead to the deaths of large numbers of the animals.

SHARING ITS HOME

Rhinos share their habitat with a number of other wild animals. Unfortunately, many of those creatures too are in danger. They are often at threat due to the same reasons the rhino is endangered.

THE ELEPHANT

Asian elephants live in parts of Asia that the rhino lives in too. That includes woodland and rain forests. The African elephant lives in places in which the rhino is also often found, such as grasslands. African elephants are bigger than Asian elephants. Asian elephants have rounder ears and smaller, straighter **tusks**. They live in swampy places during the dry season, then move into rain forest in the wet season. Both types of elephant are important keystone species. Elephants are under threat because the land they live on is being cleared for farmland and building, or used for logging. Logging is the cutting down of trees to sell the wood. Elephants are also hunted for their tusks.

THE LION

Lions live on Africa's grasslands, alongside the rhino. These magnificent predators are also at risk because of farming. Lions are also hunted illegally. Their body parts are prized and sold in the illegal wildlife trade. This is an international illegal system of selling animals and their body parts.

THE CHIMPANZEE

Chimpanzees live in Central Africa in areas of forest that rhinos roam. Chimpanzees are **endangered** because their habitat is being cut down for logging and building. It is also cleared for farming or **mining**. The animals are hunted by people for their meat. They are prized for their body parts, too, which are sold into the illegal wildlife trade. Baby chimpanzees are also captured and sold as pets or for entertainment.

THE ORANGUTAN

The orangutan is an amazing ape. It is covered with shaggy orange hair and has incredibly long arms. Orangutans live in the rain forests of Sumatra and Borneo, in Southeast Asia. Like the rhinos they live alongside, orangutans are threatened by deforestation. The rain forests in which they live are often cleared to make room for palm oil plantations. They are also cleared for mining, farming, and to make way for towns.

CHAPTER THREE

UNDER THREAT FROM HUNTING

Hunting of rhinos is a major threat to the animals. Rhinos are mainly hunted for their horns, which are cut off and sold. Rhino horns are highly prized in the illegal wildlife trade, and can be sold for a lot of money. The cost of rhino horn can be greater even than gold. That makes rhinos an attractive target for poachers.

USED FOR MEDICINE

Especially in parts of Asia, rhino horns are very valuable. That is because they are believed to have medicinal properties, or have value when made into medicines. In countries such as China and Vietnam, rhino horn is believed to treat fever and even disease such as cancer. However, the medicines the horn is made into do not work and are not based on any scientific evidence. Despite that, many people believe in them. For that reason, the selling of medicine made from rhino horn is a major driver of poaching.

▲ This rhino has had its horns removed.

"Dehorning is... a way to make the rhinos less attractive to poachers..."

Cathy Dean of Save the Rhino International

Kids on a Mission

@jay_rhinosneedus_001

If people were better educated about rhinos, and realized that medicine made from rhino horns does not work, they'd be less likely to buy it. I'm a member of the World Wildlife Fund (WWF) now.

AGAINST THE LAW

The illegal wildlife trade is the illegal trade of wild plants and animals. The business is worth billions of dollars worldwide. Some estimates put the value of the business at between $50 and $150 billion dollars a year. The value of the business is so great that poachers and sellers will go to great lengths to hunt and kill rhinos and sell their horns. They will risk being caught, because they can earn so much money working in the illegal wildlife trade. The attraction of earning money from poaching rhinos makes the job of protecting them even more difficult.

SOLD FOR STATUS

Some people buy rhino horns as status symbols, to show wealth and power. Rhino horns are very expensive to buy. If a person has one, it is a sign that they have a lot of wealth. The horns are also sometimes given as gifts. Again, because they are so expensive to buy, giving a rhino horn as a gift carries a lot of meaning. In certain communities, owning rhino horns means that people are viewed as very important.

SPOTLIGHT ON POACHING

Sadly, hunting rhinos for their horns has gone on for hundreds of years. In the nineteenth and twentieth centuries, Europeans took over more and more of Africa. At that time, hunting its animals became a sport. Since then, rhinos have mainly been hunted and killed for their horns.

TRACKING AND HUNTING

Poachers often track rhinos in their habitat by following their tracks or signs of grazing. They track rhinos both in areas outside reserves and within reserves themselves. Some poachers use tools such as **Global Positioning System (GPS)** devices to find rhinos. Sometimes, poachers are in contact with **corrupt** workers within reserves, who give them the details of rhinos that are fitted with GPS trackers. The poachers then use the GPS **coordinates** to track down those rhinos. They also use **drones** to search for the animals from the air.

▲ When rhinos are dehorned by conservationists, they are cared for and the process is carried out skilfully. The animals are monitored afterward too to make sure they are not at risk of infection.

PEOPLE ON A MISSION: CATCHING AND STOPPING POACHERS

Wildlife officers patrol areas where rhinos live to protect the animals from poachers. They use technology to help them. They fly drones with cameras over rhino territory to look out for poachers. They also use the drones to monitor rhino numbers and the movements of the animals.

Patrol officers also use sniffer dogs to track down poachers. The dogs are trained to smell the rhinos and show their handlers where they might be. Wildlife officers often wait until it is dark to catch poachers. They may find them sleeping in rhino territory, during trips to hunt and poach the animals. They then catch and arrest the poachers.

To try to stop poachers hunting rhinos and taking their horns, sometimes conservation workers remove the horns themselves. This is called dehorning. It is done safely and with **anesthetics**, so the rhinos are not harmed and do not feel any pain.

REMOVING RHINO HORNS

Once they have caught or killed a rhino, poachers use tools to remove its horn or horns as quickly as they can. Those tools often include axes, swordlike weapons called machetes, or chainsaws. Poachers often cut close to a rhino's skull, or even cut into it in order to remove as much of the horn as they can. That often severely injures the rhino, or kills it. A rhino can die from losing blood or getting an infection after its horn has been removed. Without its horn, it is less able to protect itself from predators and is easily killed.

BABY RHINOS

Poaching of female rhinos is a major problem. When a female rhino is killed, it means that the overall rhino population is likely to be further damaged.

FEW AND FAR BETWEEN

Female rhinos usually **mate** every two to five years. Mothers can be pregnant for a long time, up to 18 months. Very rarely, they have twins, or two calves. However, it is much more likely for mothers to have just one baby.

HAVING BABIES

When it is time for a mother rhino to give birth, she will find a quiet, safe place. She looks for somewhere predators will be less able to find her calf. Most rhino calves weigh about 90 to 140 pounds (40 to 65 kg) at birth. They have thick skin, like their mothers. However, the skin of a baby rhino is softer. It gets tougher as the young rhino grows.

IN DANGER

Rhino mothers spend a lot of time caring for their babies, to make sure that they survive in the wild. The babies need their mothers from the moment they are born. Calves can stand and start walking within just a few hours after birth. But they need their mother to protect them from dangers such as predators. Baby rhinos are small enough for large predators to attack. Lions, hyenas, and crocodiles all feed on rhino calves. Mothers fight off any predators that threaten their babies.

GROWING UP

Female rhinos feed their babies with milk from their bodies. This is called nursing. Calves nurse for about 12 to 18 months. Young rhinos stay with their mother until they are about two or three years old. At that point, they leave their mothers and find their own territory. Female rhinos will be ready to have babies of their own when they are about five to seven years old. Males do not normally reproduce until they are seven to ten years old.

CHAPTER FOUR

CLIMATE CHANGE THREATS

Climate change is one of the greatest threats to life on our planet. This threat does not just pose a danger to humans, it also threatens rhinos and other wildlife. As Earth's temperature increases, our planet is seeing greater changes in its weather patterns. This affects every organism on Earth.

WHAT IS CLIMATE CHANGE?

Climate change is a change in temperature or weather in an area over a period of time. Climate change has always happened slowly throughout Earth's history, due to natural factors such as changes in the sun and **geological** activity. However, the climate change we are experiencing today is largely caused by human activities. These include burning **fossil fuels**, which releases gases into Earth's **atmosphere**. These gases circle the planet like a blanket, causing it to heat up.

◀ A protective blanket of gases surrounds our planet—the atmosphere. The gases we pump from our car exhausts and from factories are changing the atmosphere.

"Rhinos have survived for millions of years but are now at risk due to our actions."

Dr Richard Leakey, conservationist

◀ When water sources that rhinos rely on dry up, the animals have no choice but to travel to new places in search of water.

Kids on a Mission

@elliot_climatechange_26

It's up to everyone to change how they live to help protect the planet. I cycle to school rather than taking the bus or car. That will help stop harmful gases getting into the atmosphere.

DROUGHTS AND FLOODS

As Earth's temperatures increase and changes in rainfall take place, that is affecting the vegetation that grows in rhino habitats. Less rainfall and increased temperatures in parts of Africa are causing long droughts. These are periods of time with little or no rainfall. During droughts the water sources rhinos depend on dry up. The animals then do not have water to drink or wallow in. The plants they depend on for food also do not grow. In other places, such as parts of Asia, climate change is causing extreme weather events, such as floods. During floods, a lot of water covers normally dry land. Floods often accompany times of increased rainfall. Floods destroy habitats and damage a region's delicate ecosystems.

SPOTLIGHT ON FLOODS

Flooding can be as devastating as droughts. Floods can cause severe soil erosion, which means the layers of soil that cover the ground are swept away by floodwaters. When soil is swept away, the important nutrients it contains are also removed. Plants need those nutrients to grow, so soil erosion results in fewer plants growing in an area. Floodwaters rip away vegetation along with soil. That immediately removes the food source of rhinos. Without soil, larger plants such as trees also cannot grow. Rhinos need them for shelter.

▲ These rhinos have been forced to higher land during a flood in India.

RHINOS UNDER STRESS

When floods hit, rhinos are forced to move to higher ground. They have to leave their home range, which disrupts their normal feeding patterns. They have to find new sources of water. That stops them gathering at their usual water holes, where they form social bonds. That all causes a lot of stress for the animals. Then, if they are forced into greater contact with people, and conflicts result, rhinos are placed under even greater stress. The normal territory boundaries of male rhinos are lost too when they are forced to move. The males are then more likely to fight. Baby and young rhinos are also at greater risk during floods. They can be swept away by floodwaters and killed.

◀ **Satellite** images, such as this image of the Namibia desert in Africa, provide detail about large areas of a landscape and possible changes to it.

PEOPLE ON A MISSION: STUDYING CLIMATE CHANGE

Climate change and environmental scientists study climate change. They note how it affects different habitats, and the organisms in them. These scientists are closely monitoring the effect of climate change on rhinos. Scientists use satellite images to study rhino habitats from above. That helps them build up a picture of how a habitat is changing due to the effects of climate change, such as increased floods and drought. Satellite images can show changes in vegetation and the availability of water. It can show alterations to the landscape caused by flooding or drought. Satellites are also used to track long-term climate information, such as temperature and rainfall. That helps scientists figure out if there are likely to be further periods of drought or flooding.

Scientists also use technology to help them figure out how climate change might affect rhinos. They put data about climate change and rhinos into a computer, which then creates different possible outcomes based on that information. That might include how the animals' habitat is likely to change. It may include how the behavior of rhinos may differ as a response to those changes.

Campaigners are also working hard to alert people to the dangers of climate change. They raise awareness of the effect it is having on rhinos and their habitats. The more aware both ordinary people and people in organizations and governments are about the impact of climate change on the natural world, the more likely they will be to take actions to try and prevent it.

RHINOS NEED WATER HOLES

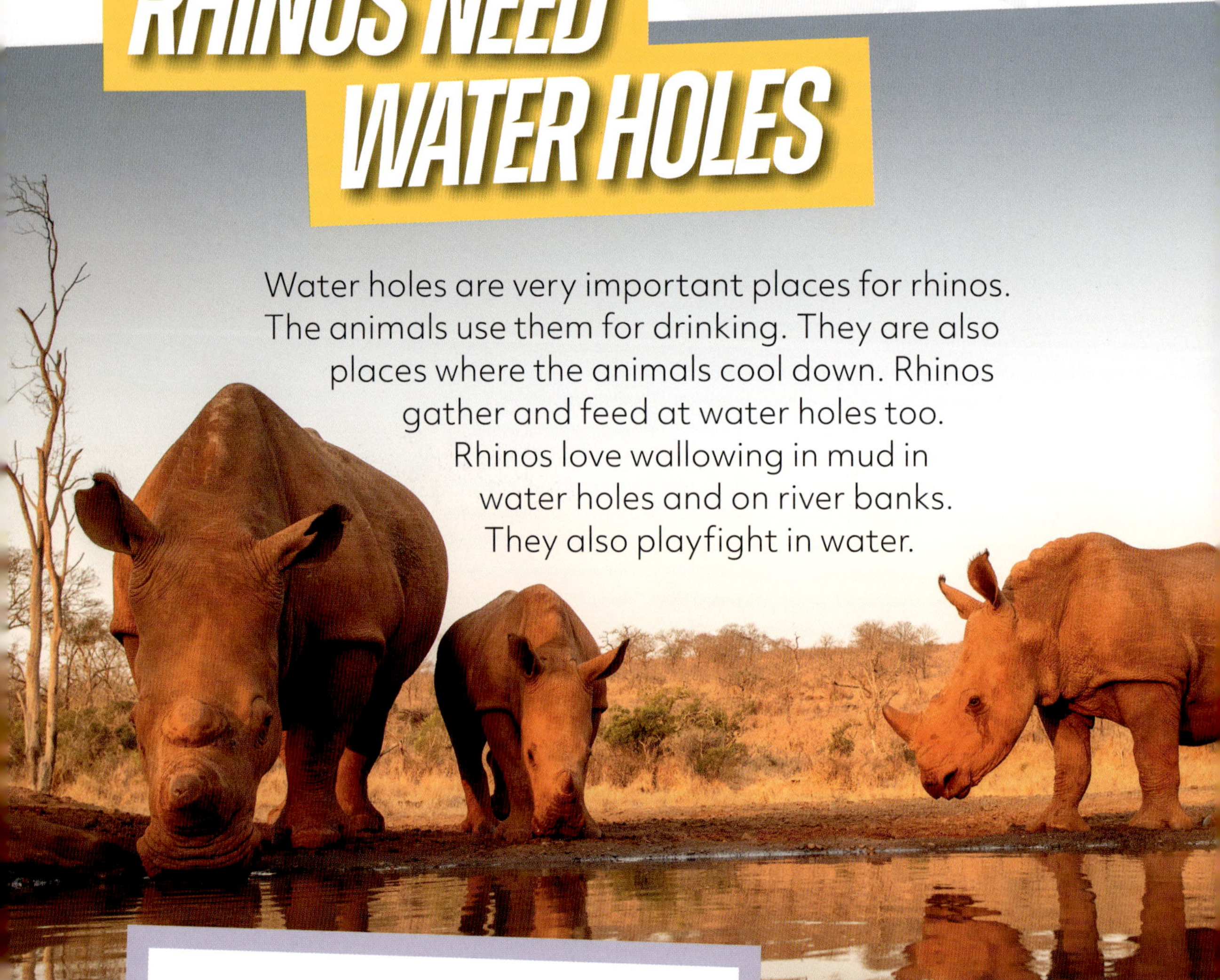

Water holes are very important places for rhinos. The animals use them for drinking. They are also places where the animals cool down. Rhinos gather and feed at water holes too. Rhinos love wallowing in mud in water holes and on river banks. They also playfight in water.

DRINKING AND EATING

Rhinos need to drink a lot of water. These big animals can drink up to 17.6 gallons (80 l) of water a day, especially when temperatures are high. If necessary, they can survive several days without water. Plants that rhinos eat also grow near water holes. The animals come to the water sources to feast on the rich vegetation that grows there, which provides them with important nutrients.

MUD PROTECTION

Rhinos have thick skin, which can easily become overheated. Wallowing in water or mud helps to regulate the body temperature of the animals. It also helps keep rhino skin moist, which stops it drying out when the weather becomes very hot. Mud also acts as a natural sunscreen. Rhinos can easily become sunburned, so wallowing helps prevent this. Mud also acts as a barrier against insects, such as ticks and flies. That helps stop rhinos becoming bitten and infected by insects.

A PLACE TO CHILL OUT

Water holes also provide adult rhinos with important places in which they can relax. Wallowing is a great way for rhinos to take a break from searching for food and just rest up for a while. That relaxation is important for their well-being.

A SAFE PLACE FOR BABIES TO LEARN

Water holes are great places for calves. While in a gathering of rhinos, calves are in less danger from predators while near the water. Mothers also take their calves to water holes to show them where to drink and how to wallow. Babies learn important social skills in water holes. There, they often playfight. That helps them form bonds with other rhinos. By playfighting, young rhinos also learn how to protect themselves and defend their territory.

CHAPTER FIVE

OTHER CHALLENGES

Rhinos face many threats, including habitat loss and damage, hunting, and climate change. But there are other issues too that are putting these magnificent animals at even greater risk.

Rhinos are big animals ▶ that need to move freely.

"The fight for rhinos is a fight for all wildlife. If we don't protect them, we may soon find ourselves losing much more than just rhinos."

Will Travers, president of the Born Free Foundation

KEPT IN CAPTIVITY

There are many zoos in the world that try to properly care for **captive** rhinos. However, some zoos do not provide rhinos with the environment and care that they need. Rhinos need a lot of space to roam and graze in. In small enclosures, rhinos are restricted. That can make them very stressed. Concrete floors rather than soil or grass can also cause foot and joint injuries. Rhinos are designed for softer, natural landscapes such as grasslands.

Without their natural habitat, rhinos can also become bored and further stressed. They show that stress in behavior such as pacing, head swinging, and scratching. Rhinos may also become stressed from too much exposure to crowds in zoos. That can lead to **anxiety** and **aggression** in the animals.

HOME INVADERS

Invasive species are plants and animals that are not naturally found in an environment. Rhinos are threatened by invasive species such as wild boars. These animals have been deliberately introduced by humans, so they can hunt the boars for sport. They also use them to control pests such as beetles, which eat farmers' crops. Wild boars feast on insects. The boars are also a problem because they compete with rhinos for food and living space. The animals carry diseases that can harm rhinos, too.

Kids on a Mission

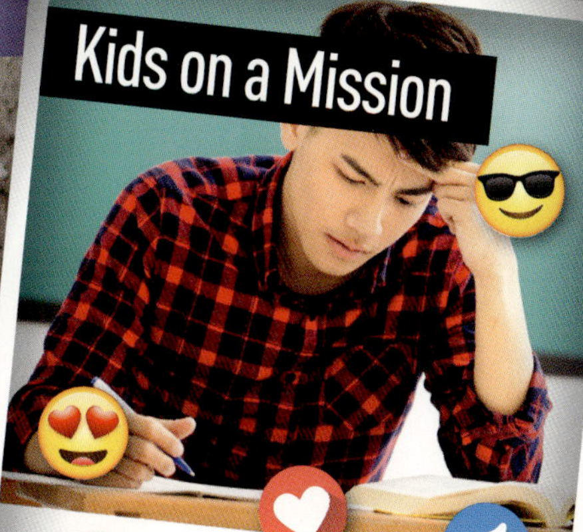

@jason_rhinorescue_108

I didn't realize that some zoos are bad for animals until I joined the Born Free Foundation. My teacher and class are now helping me raise money for the Foundation, so it can stop rhinos being held in harmful captivity.

RHINOS AND WAR

Unfortunately, rhinos live in places where there is a lot of war and conflict. These clashes can damage the animals' habitats, and put the rhinos at great risk. Wars in parts of Africa have damaged rhino populations. In all areas, rhinos have been killed or forced to leave their territories due to fighting. Conflicts in parts of Asia have also harmed rhinos.

SPOTLIGHT ON WAR

War and conflict has a devastating effect on people, but it also can be terrible for animals such as rhinos. Conflict leads to even further destruction of their habitat. It makes it more difficult for rangers to monitor rhinos safely. Just as war forces people to move from their homes, it also forces rhinos to move from theirs. That displacement puts the animals at risk because it can affect their supply of food, water, and shelter.

THE DANGER OF CONFLICT

When armies or groups of fighters use fire, bombs, and **land mines**, they damage natural environments. Vehicles travel across rhino territory, further damaging it. All that activity forces rhinos into new areas—where they may be at greater risk from poachers.

In conflict zones, the laws that might protect animals in peacetime often break down. That means illegal activities such as poaching become a lot easier. Armed groups often use poaching as a means of funding their operations. Selling rhino horns raises a lot of money, which can be used to buy **military** equipment.

▲ Rhinos face greater risks than ever during wartime. Even protected areas that once may have provided some safety can become very dangerous.

◀ Protecting rhinos and following conservation laws often becomes even less of a focus when war breaks out.

PEOPLE ON A MISSION: RHINO PROTECTORS

Protecting rhinos during wartime is a huge challenge. To try to help the animals, conservation organizations often need to increase the amount of money they make available to conservation. That money may be used to train more rangers and fund more equipment to help track rhinos. With increased poaching of rhinos during wartime, the animals need even more support.

When war breaks out in places near rhino territory, conservationists may move the animals to areas where they will be safer. That is called translocation. It can be a huge undertaking because it may mean moving rhinos hundreds of miles away. That is also very stressful for the rhinos, but it may be necessary to save their lives. Conservation organizations may also work with international governments to raise awareness of what is happening to rhinos in war-torn areas. They bring pressure to make sure that people still follow wildlife protection laws.

After fighting has ended, more effort is needed to help rhinos. Rebuilding rhino populations and habitats is important work. That might mean returning rhinos to areas they were moved from. It can also mean reintroducing new rhinos to those habitats, to try and rebuild the population. Restoring habitats damaged by war is vital. That can include rebuilding protected areas that have been harmed as a result of the conflict.

RHINO RELATIVES IN DANGER

Several relatives of the rhino are also at threat, largely because of the actions of humans. These animals are losing their homes due to farming, building, and climate change. Some are also threatened by hunting.

THE TAPIR

Tapirs are closely related to rhinos. They are sometimes named "living **fossils**." That is because they have lived on Earth for millions of years, but changed very little in that time. The animals have a round body, short legs, and a short tail. Their most unusual feature is their prehensile snout. They use it like a small trunk to grip leaves, fruit, and branches for food.

Tapirs live in forests in Southeast Asia, and are also found in forests in parts of Central and South America. Their habitat is being cleared due to logging, farming, and to make way for land to build on. The animals are hunted by local people for their meat. They are also hunted for their body parts, which are used in some traditional medicines.

GREVY'S ZEBRA

Grevy's Zebra is the most endangered of all zebra species. The animal lives in Kenya and Ethiopia in Africa, alongside rhinos that live in grassland there. Like the rhino, the zebra is threatened because it has lost a lot of its habitat due to farming and building. As farming spreads across the animal's territory and roads cut through it too, it is difficult for the zebras to follow their usual **migration** routes. Zebras migrate large distances to find food and water. During dry seasons, vegetation is reduced in their grassland home ranges. The zebras then move to areas where it has rained recently and there is more food to eat. When water sources dry up in grasslands during dry seasons, zebras migrate to other areas of water created by seasonal rains.

THE AFRICAN WILD ASS

The African wild ass is a critically endangered animal that lives in Africa. It is mainly found in the countries of Eritrea and Ethiopia. The ass is hunted for its meat and skin. Like the rhino, the ass reproduces very slowly, so any loss of its numbers badly damages the population. The habitat of these animals is being damaged by farming. Another danger is that farmers often kill the asses when they come into contact with them. That is because they believe the animals are feeding on grassland that they need for their livestock. However, too much livestock grazing on the natural habitat of the ass is reducing the amount of food available to these wild creatures. The existence of the wild ass is now at risk.

WHAT'S NEXT FOR THE RHINO?

The work of dedicated conservationists is helping rhinos around the world. They have brought the fate of the rhino to the attention of people everywhere. Governments too are taking actions to help rhinos in countries in which they are threatened. But much more needs to be done if we are to save rhinos, particularly species that are in great danger, such as the northern white rhino. There are now just two females left in the wild.

HELP FROM CONSERVATIONISTS

Conservationists are playing a crucial part in protecting rhinos in their habitats. They are creating more protected areas in which the animals can live. They are also creating habitat corridors. These are safe areas between rhino territories. The corridors pass through areas of farmland, for example, so that rhinos can safely travel across them. That helps rhinos move between areas to meet other rhinos and mate. The method is helping increase and protect rhino populations. It also means that rhinos can move more safely in search of food and water.

"Rhinos are a **keystone species**; they inspire hope."

Dr Susie Ellis of the International Rhino Foundation (IRF)

HELP FROM ORGANIZATIONS

Many organizations around the world are working hard to help protect rhinos. The WWF in particular plays an important role in rhino protection. It helps fund ranger training. It also supplies rangers with important equipment, such as GPS-tracking devices and drones that help track and monitor rhinos. The WWF also leads public education campaigns in countries where rhino horn is in great demand, such as Vietnam and China. The campaigns try to educate people about traditional medicine. Organizations are also doing all they can to protect the rhino's environment from the dangers it faces.

HELP FROM ALL OF US

Everyone can do a lot to help rhinos, too. We can all raise awareness of the dangers of habitat loss and the threat of the illegal wildlife trade. By living more sustainably, we can help reduce the impact we are having on climate change. We can educate as many people as we can about the dangers rhinos face, and what we all can do to help them. Rhinos are amazing animals, but they need our help if they are to still roam on Earth for years to come.

Kids on a Mission

@sophia_rhinoSOS_now1

Through the WWF I've found out about the work of rangers. I want to be a ranger and work with rhinos in Africa. That would be amazing.

MAKE IT YOUR MISSION: A CAREER IN CONSERVATION

Many people who are passionate about protecting rhinos and other endangered animals build a career in that field. On pages 44–45 you'll find some of the conservation careers you could pursue, if that is your dream. Below are ideas for things you can do right now to prepare for a career in conservation and help save rhinos.

GET SET TO STUDY

Working hard at school now will pay off if you want a conservation career. Pay attention in your science, English, and geography classes. Languages are also useful. If you have a job overseas, being able to speak a foreign language is helpful.

GET CONNECTED

Connecting with other people who care about wildlife is a great way to feel empowered about saving endangered animals. You'll find some of the organizations you can join on page 47. By connecting with other people who are concerned about the environment, you'll find out what you can do to help. Being involved with conservation organizations and charities now will also help you when you apply for jobs in the future. It will show that you have been interested in conservation from an early age.

▲ Find out all you can about rhinos, and spread the word! The more people are aware of rhinos and the difficulties they face, the better placed everyone will be to help them.

GET EXPERIENCE

Any form of work experience in wildlife care will be useful for a future conservation career. Why not apply to local zoos, charities, and conservation organizations as soon as you are old enough?

TAKE ACTION!

You'll have learned about some of the actions that help rhinos from the Kids on a Mission features in this book. Here are some more ideas for other activities that can help protect rhinos:

- Adopt a rhino! There are many wildlife protection organizations that offer rhino adoption as a way of helping these animals. Take a look at the WWF, IRF, and Save the Rhino International. There are other sites too. Ask your parents to help you.
- Never go to a zoo that keeps rhinos in close captivity. Remember, rhinos should have room to roam.
- Educate yourself and others about rhinos. Watch good-quality television shows about rhinos, and read great books about them, like this one! Tell your family and friends about what you have learned and encourage them to find out more. The better informed people are about rhinos, the more they'll want to help them.
- Ask your school to hold a fundraising event to raise money for an organization such as IRF or the Born Free Foundation.
- Start a blog about rhinos and the dangers they face. Educate as many people as you can.

Climate change is an issue that is affecting ▶ each and every one of us. Many young people are campaigning to call for governmental changes that will slow down the threat.

CAREERS IN CONSERVATION

There are many different types of conservation careers. The one you choose depends on your specific areas of interest and your particular talents and skills. Here is information about some of them. You can find out about other conservation jobs on page 47 of this book.

▲ Wildlife **biologists** use tools such as hidden or remote cameras to record and monitor animal behavior in their natural environment.

ZOOLOGIST

A zoologist is a scientist who specializes in studying animals. In this role, you might study one species or a group of species. Zoologists who study rhinos conduct research to find out more about what the animals need to survive. This knowledge helps protect a species, and it helps manage how it adjusts to issues such as climate change and habitat loss.

WILDLIFE MANAGER

If you became a wildlife manager, you would work with wild animals and wild habitats. You would do a variety of jobs. They would include supervising hunting within an area and keeping track of the animal populations there. You would also make sure that the habitat is suitable for the animals in it. You might work with local people to encourage communities to help protect the animals. Most wildlife managers have a degree in environmental studies.

WILDLIFE TECHNICIAN

Wildlife technicians study wildlife in its natural habitat. They closely watch animal numbers and animal behavior. In this role you might work for **resource** companies, governments, and environmental firms. They help ensure that wildlife protection laws are followed. A degree in wildlife management is usually required for this role.

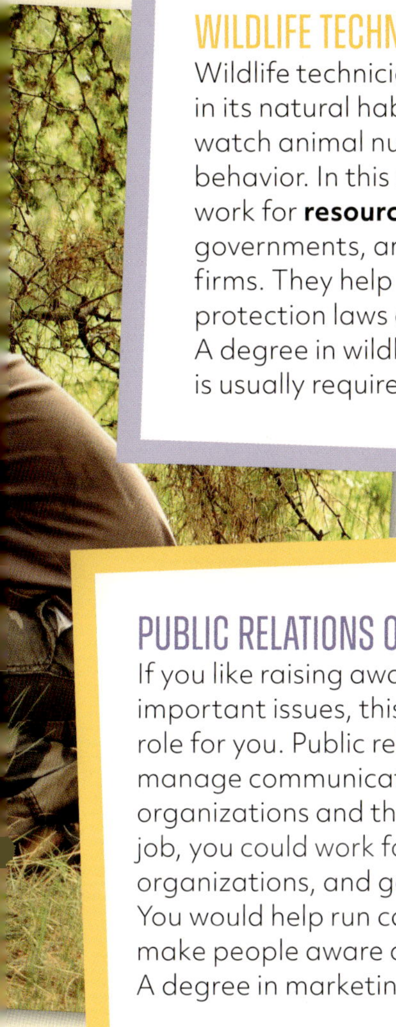

WILDLIFE ECONOMIST

Are you good at math? Some mathematicians work as wildlife economists. They assess ecosystems and figure out their value to people. They literally put a price on habitats and animals. That information can be used to persuade governments and companies to protect them.

PUBLIC RELATIONS OFFICER

If you like raising awareness about important issues, this could be the role for you. Public relations officers manage communications between organizations and the public. In this job, you could work for charities, organizations, and governments. You would help run campaigns to make people aware of wildlife issues. A degree in marketing is useful.

JOBS IN ECOTOURISM

If you took up a career in ecotourism you would work with people and show them the natural world. You would do so in ways that are sustainable and do not negatively impact wildlife or habitats. Ecotourism is a very important part of conservation efforts in many countries, because it encourages people to care about the natural world. The money tourists pay also provides funds to protect habitats and animals.

◀ Ecotourism is a growing industry.

GLOSSARY

aggression unfriendly behavior
anesthetics drugs that make a living creature unconscious, so it does not feel pain
anxiety feeling very scared, worried, or frightened
atmosphere the blanket of gases that surrounds Earth
biologists scientists who study biology
captive held in a confined area, not free
climate change a shift in the average weather conditions on Earth
communications the sharing of messages of information
conservation the protection of the planet
conservationists people who try and protect the planet
coordinates numbers that show the location of something
corrupt not trustworthy
critically endangered facing an extremely high risk of extinction in the wild
drones unmanned flying vehicles often used to track and observe things from the sky
endangered facing a very high risk of extinction in the wild
environment a natural place where plants and animals live
extinction dying out
fossil fuels fuels formed from the remains of plants and animals that lived long ago
fossils hardened remains of plants and animals that lived long ago
geological related to Earth's structure
Global Positioning System (GPS) a system of satellites in space around Earth that send us information about our planet
grassland a wide-open area of grass with few shrubs and trees
habitat the place in which a plant or animal lives
keystone species an animal or plant that has a big impact on its ecosystem. If a keystone species disappears, the whole ecosystem could change dramatically or even collapse
land mines bombs hidden beneath the surface of the ground that are triggered when they are touched
mate to breed in order to produce offspring
migration the movement of an animal or group of animals over distance, often to find food or water
military fighting forces
mining the process of digging into the ground to extract, or take out, resources within it
organisms living creatures
poached hunted illegally
pollution substances that are harmful to living things
population all of the organisms belonging to one species and living in one place
prehensile adapted, or changed, for seizing and gripping
preserving keeping safe
rain forests areas of trees that receive at least 100 inches (254 cm) of rain each year
resource something that is needed or desired
satellite an object in space that circles another object, such as a planet
scrubland land covered with woody, dry plants called scrub
sense one of the five senses of sight, hearing, smell, touch, and taste
species a type of plant or animal
swamps areas of land mainly covered with shallow water in which water-living plants and animals thrive
territory an area of land that humans or other animals regard as their own
tropical describes areas that are frost-free all year around and with consistently warm temperatures
tusks very long, large teeth
vegetation plants
wetlands areas of land that are covered with shallow water

FIND OUT MORE

BOOKS

Jenkins, Martin. *Endangered Animals*. Walker Studio, 2024.

Kellett, Jenny. Rhinos: *The Ultimate Rhino Book* (Animal Books for Kids). Bellanova Books, 2022.

Spilsbury, Louise. *Saving the Asian Elephant* (Mission Survival: Saving Earth's Endangered Animals). Cheriton Children's Books, 2023.

WEBSITES

Discover more about careers that help fight climate change at:
www.bestcolleges.com/blog/climate-change-jobs

Hear directly from people working in conservation! Find out what they have to say about working in a career in conservation at:
www.conservation-careers.com/conservation-jobs-careers-advice/how-to-get-a-job-in-conservation

Discover the ultimate guide to careers in conservation at:
www.conservation-careers.com/15-key-conservation-jobs-ultimate-guide-for-conservation-job-seekers

Discover careers in environmental science at:
https://jobs.environmentalscience.org

Learn more about rhinos at the IRF website:
https://rhinos.org

Discover more about rhinos and how to help save them at Save the Rhino International:
www.savetherhino.org

Publisher's note to educators and parents:
All the websites featured above have been carefully reviewed to ensure that they are suitable for students. However, many websites change often, and we cannot guarantee that a site's future contents will continue to meet our high standards of educational value. Please be advised that students should be closely monitored whenever they access the Internet.

INDEX

ABOUT THE AUTHOR

Sarah Eason has written a number of books on animals and the dangers they face. In researching this book, she has realized why people love rhinos so much, how important these animals are, and why everyone should try and help save them.